Going on a Train

by Sue Graves and Irene Montano

W
FRANKLIN WATTS
LONDON•SYDNEY

We are going on a train ride.

We go to the train station.

We need tickets
to get on the train.

We buy the tickets.

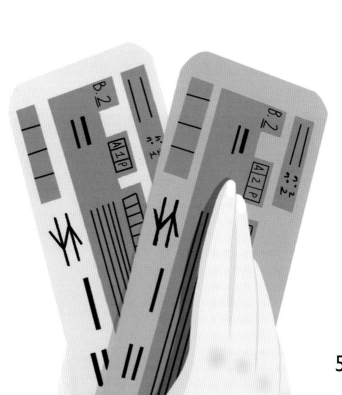

We go to the platform.

We get some sweets
to eat on the train.

We can see lots of trains.
This train carries coal.

This train carries people.

We wait for the train.

We do not have to wait long.

The train stops
and we get on.

We look for a seat.

We sit by the window.

The train gets faster
and faster.

We look out of the window.

We see cows and sheep.

The train stops at the station and we get off.

The train ride was fun!

Talk and Explore

Ask your child to describe each picture below, in their own words, pointing to each picture in turn.

Discuss the different stages of going on a train journey and what to expect at each stage.

Independent Reading

This series is designed to provide an opportunity for your child to read on their own. These notes are written for you to help your child choose a book and to read it independently.

In school, your child's teacher will often be using reading books which have been banded to support the process of learning to read.

Use the book band colour your child is reading in school to help you make a good choice. *Going on a Train* is a good choice for children reading at Yellow Band in their classroom to read independently.

The aim of independent reading is to read this book with ease, so that your child enjoys the story and relates it to their own experiences.

About the book

This book reports on the experience of going on a train for the first time.

Before reading

Help your child to learn how to make good choices by asking:
"Why did you choose this book? Why do you think you will enjoy it?" Look at the cover together and ask: "What do you think the book will be about?" Support your child to think of what they already know about the story context. Read the title aloud and ask: "What do you think the adult and child are going to do? Where are they? Why do you think that?" Remind your child that they can try to sound out the letters to make a word if they get stuck.

Decide together whether your child will read the story independently or read it aloud to you. When books are short, as at Yellow Band, your child may wish to do both!

During reading

If reading aloud, support your child if they hesitate or ask for help by telling the word. Remind your child of what they know and what they can do independently.

If reading to themselves, remind your child that they can come and ask for your help if stuck.

After reading

Support understanding of the book by asking your child to tell you what they found out. Did they learn anything new? Did anything surprise them?

As you discuss the book, you might begin to use vocabulary such as station, platform, ticket, seat, railway and tracks.

Give your child a chance to respond to the book: "Have you travelled on a train before? What was similar and what was different to the train journey in this book?"

Use the Talk and Explore activity to encourage your child to talk about what they have learned.

Extending learning

Talk about what you need to do before you get on a train. Think about all the different reasons people use trains. Make a list of all the different types of train you can think of and what they are used for. Create a simple step-by-step guide for someone going on a passenger train for the first time.

In the classroom, your child's teacher may be introducing punctuation.On a few of the pages, check your child can recognise capital letters and full stops by asking them to point these out.

Franklin Watts
First published in Great Britain in 2021
by The Watts Publishing Group

Series Editors: Jackie Hamley and Melanie Palmer
Development Editors and Series Advisors: Dr Sue Bodman and Glen Franklin
Series Designers: Cathryn Gilbert and Peter Scoulding

A CIP catalogue record for this book is
available from the British Library.

ISBN 978 1 4451 7678 9 (hbk)
ISBN 978 1 4451 7680 2 (pbk)
ISBN 978 1 4451 7679 6 (library ebook)
ISBN 978 1 4451 8339 8 (ebook)

Printed in China

Franklin Watts
An imprint of
Hachette Children's Group
Part of The Watts Publishing Group
Carmelite House
50 Victoria Embankment
London EC4Y 0DZ

An Hachette UK Company
www.hachette.co.uk

www.franklinwatts.co.uk